Claude 3 & 3.5 Crash Course:

Business Applications and API

Greg Lim

Table of Contents

Preface

About this book

In this book, we take you on a fun, hands-on and pragmatic journey to learning how to use Claude 3.5 for business applications and build apps with the Claude API. You'll learn how to use Claude features like Artifacts and Projects within minutes. Every section is written in a bite-sized manner and straight to the point as I don't want to waste your time (and most certainly mine) on the content you don't need.

In the course of this book, we will cover:
- Chapter 1: Introduction to Claude 3 and 3.5
- Chapter 2: Claude UI, Applications and Features
- Chapter 3: Claude Artifacts
- Chapter 4: Introduction to Claude Projects
- Chapter 5: Enchancing Instructions for Project Performance
- Chapter 6: Introduction to Claude API

The goal of this book is to teach you to use Claude in a practical way without overwhelming you. We focus only on the essentials and cover the material in a hands-on practice manner for you to follow along.

Getting Book Updates

To receive updated versions of the book, subscribe to our mailing list by sending a mail to support@i-ducate.com. I try to update my books to use the latest version of software, libraries and will update the codes/content in this book. So do subscribe to my list to receive updated copies!

Contact and Code Examples

Contact me at support@i-ducate.com to obtain the source files used in this book. Comments or questions concerning this book can also be directed to the same.

Chapter 1: Introduction to Claude 3 and 3.5

Anthropic Claude 3 and 3.5, a rising star among LLMs, has exceptionally high performance and even surpasses other GPT models.

Its key strengths include:
- exceptional code generation
- proficient writing and content creation
- effective marketing assistance
- versatile applications across various domains

As of writing this book, Claude 3.5 Sonnet stands out as the best available model for general public use.

This book will guide you through the world of Claude, focusing on its latest iterations: Claude 3 and 3.5. We will:
- have a high level overview of what Claude is
- increase efficiency through features and applications of Claude 3 and 3.5, like Artifacts and Projects,
- explore the Claude 3 API for developers, where we see how to use the Claude API in our apps. As an example, we will build a Handwriting-Analysis app using this API.

We're excited to embark on this journey with you! Whether you're looking to boost your personal productivity or integrate Claude AI capabilities into your applications, this book has something valuable for everyone.

Let's dive in and unlock the full potential of Claude 3 and 3.5.

What is Claude?

It's easy to get confused because Claude refers to both a UI front end (the user interface) and the name of the backend model. Essentially, Claude is an AI model developed by Anthropic, the company behind Claude.
- It's designed to understand not just text, but also images and documents, making it a multimodal model that can accept multiple types of input and provide answers in various formats.
- Claude excels in natural language processing tasks such as conversation, content creation, and virtual assistance.

When you visit the Claude website at claude.ai, what you see is Claude's user interface:

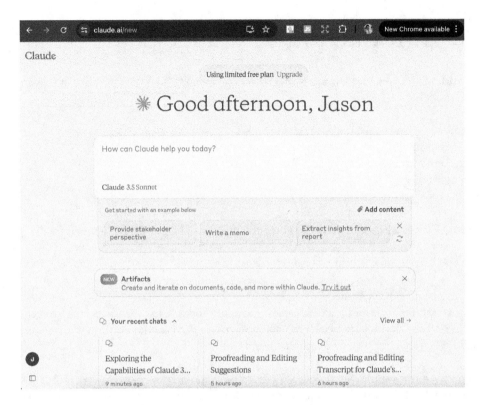

When you type something in the UI, Claude sends a request to the backend model you're using. For example, I'm currently using Claude 3.5 Sonnet:

If you are using the Free plan, you only have access to Claude 3.5 Sonnet (the Free Plan uses the same model as the Premium version, so the response quality should be similar).

If you sign up for the Pro plan, you can access the different model options: 3.5 Sonnet, 3 Opus, and 3 Haiku.

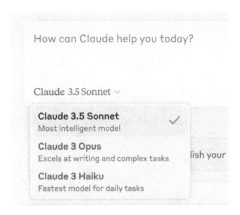

Note: Don't worry about selecting a specific model at the moment (we'll introduce them in more depth later). The default model, Claude 3.5 Sonnet, is Anthropic's newest model (as of the time of writing this book) and is designed to understand and create text better than previous versions.

The Evolution of Claude: From 1.0 to 3.5

Claude 3 or 3.5 is not the first version of this AI model. There have been several legacy versions of Claude, including Claude Instant 1.2, Claude 2, and Claude 2.1. (For full details, see: https://docs.anthropic.com/en/docs/about-claude/models)

The initial model was Claude 1, a basic text-to-text generation model. Then they announced Claude Instant 1.1 (and later 1.2). These were foundational models that weren't as widely recognized as today's Claude 3.5.

Claude 2 marked a significant improvement, being faster and more advanced than previous versions. It performed better on benchmarks, which led to increased publicity as it compared favorably to GPT-3 and GPT-3.5.

The announcement of Claude 3 Sonnet, Haiku, and Opus (the Claude 3 series) catapulted Claude to widespread popularity. These models even outperformed GPT-4 on certain benchmarks.

The latest iteration, Claude 3.5 Sonnet, surpassed GPT-4o in both speed and performance, making it the most advanced model available at the time of writing.

Understanding Claude 3.5 Sonnet

Claude 3.5 Sonnet represents the latest model family in the Claude series. It's designed to be multimodal, similar to the Claude 3 models. It's part of a family that includes other models like Claude 3 Opus and Claude 3 Haiku, which users can select in the Claude UI (under the Pro plan):

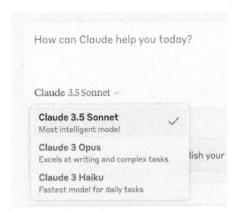

Claude 3 Haiku is the least powerful, but the fastest in the series. Claude 3 Opus (previously the most advanced version) is the high end model with powerful capabilities, but Claude 3.5 Sonnet is faster and more capable than Claude 3 Opus.

To fully appreciate the capabilities of Claude 3.5 Sonnet, let's examine the official Claude 3.5 documentation for a high-level overview of its benchmark performance:

Claude 3.5 Sonnet is now available for free on Claude.ai and the Claude iOS app, while Claude Pro and Team plan subscribers can access it with significantly higher rate limits. It is also available via the Anthropic API, Amazon Bedrock, and Google Cloud's Vertex AI. The model costs $3 per million input tokens and $15 per million output tokens, with a 200K token context window.

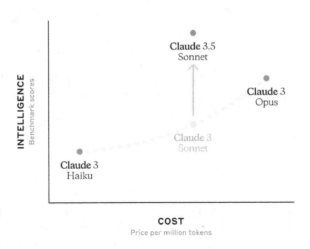

(https://www.anthropic.com/news/claude-3-5-sonnet)

The model is currently available on Amazon Bedrock and Google Cloud Vertex AI. It costs approximately $3 per million input tokens and $15 per million output tokens. Input tokens are what you send to the model, such as prompts or input text, while output tokens are generated by the model in its responses.

Claude 3.5 Sonnet has a 200,000 input token context window (about 500 pages of material), meaning it can understand very long text and maintain consistency throughout the conversation history. This is one of the longest context windows available today (GPT-4o has a 128,000 token context window). Currently, Gemini 1.5 has the largest token context window at 1 million tokens.

Regarding intelligence benchmarks, Claude 3.5 Sonnet outperforms both its predecessor (Claude 3) and Claude 3 Opus. Interestingly, it is also more cost-effective than Opus. As a result, Opus is currently the most expensive model in the Claude family, despite being less intelligent than Claude 3.5 Sonnet:

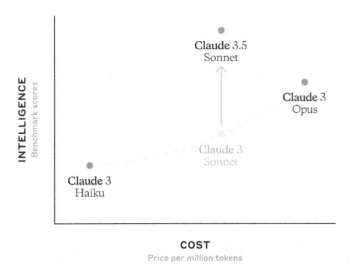

Claude 3.5 Opus, when released, will likely surpass Claude 3.5 in terms of intelligence. However, it's also expected to be more expensive than Claude 3.5 due to increased generation processing time.

According to the benchmark chart shared on Anthropic's page (shown below), Claude 3.5 outperforms GPT-4o in several areas. This is a significant achievement, as few models today can claim such performance against GPT-4o:

	Claude 3.5 Sonnet	Claude 3 Opus	GPT-4o	Gemini 1.5 Pro	Llama-400b (early snapshot)
Graduate level reasoning *GPQA, Diamond*	59.4%* 0-shot CoT	50.4% 0-shot CoT	53.6% 0-shot CoT	—	—
Undergraduate level knowledge *MMLU*	88.7%** 5-shot	86.8% 5-shot	—	85.9% 5-shot	86.1% 5-shot
	88.3% 0-shot CoT	85.7% 0-shot CoT	88.7% 0-shot CoT	—	—
Code *HumanEval*	92.0% 0-shot	84.9% 0-shot	90.2% 0-shot	84.1% 0-shot	84.1% 0-shot
Multilingual math *MGSM*	91.6% 0-shot CoT	90.7% 0-shot CoT	90.5% 0-shot CoT	87.5% 8-shot	—
Reasoning over text *DROP, F1 score*	87.1 3-shot	83.1 3-shot	83.4 3-shot	74.9 Variable shots	83.5 3-shot Pre-trained model
Mixed evaluations *BIG-Bench-Hard*	93.1% 3-shot CoT	86.8% 3-shot CoT	—	89.2% 3-shot CoT	85.3% 3-shot CoT Pre-trained model
Math problem-solving *MATH*	71.1% 0-shot CoT	60.1% 0-shot CoT	76.6% 0-shot CoT	67.7% 4-shot	57.8% 4-shot CoT
Grade school math *GSM8K*	96.4% 0-shot CoT	95.0% 0-shot CoT	—	90.8% 11-shot	94.1% 8-shot CoT

* Claude 3.5 Sonnet scores 67.2% on 5-shot CoT GPQA with maj@32
** Claude 3.5 Sonnet scores 90.4% on MMLU with 5-shot CoT prompting

On the MMLU (Massive Multitask Language Understanding) benchmark, which focuses on mathematical reasoning, Claude outperforms all other models in the 5-shot prompting scenario:

	Claude 3.5 Sonnet	Claude 3 Opus	GPT-4o	Gemini 1.5 Pro	Llama-400b (early snapshot)
Graduate level reasoning *GPQA, Diamond*	59.4%* 0-shot CoT	50.4% 0-shot CoT	53.6% 0-shot CoT	—	—
Undergraduate level knowledge *MMLU*	88.7%** 5-shot	86.8% 5-shot	—	85.9% 5-shot	86.1% 5-shot
	88.3% 0-shot CoT	85.7% 0-shot CoT	88.7% 0-shot CoT	—	—

GPT-4o is not benchmarked here. 5-shot is when you give 5 examples and then expect the model to solve the problem. Claude 3.5 does better than all the benchmarks available at this point in time, but it falls short of GPT-4o when it comes to zero-shot prompting.

*Zero-shot prompting is when you don't provide any examples to the model, yet it's able to answer correctly.

In terms of coding capabilities, Claude 3.5 Sonnet performs exceptionally well. The benchmarks indicate it's nearly 2% better than GPT-4o in this area.

	Claude 3.5 Sonnet	Claude 3 Opus	GPT-4o	Gemini 1.5 Pro	Llama-400b (early snapshot)
Graduate level reasoning GPQA, Diamond	59.4%* 0-shot CoT	50.4% 0-shot CoT	53.6% 0-shot CoT	—	—
Undergraduate level knowledge MMLU	88.7%** 5-shot	86.8% 5-shot	—	85.9% 5-shot	86.1% 5-shot
	88.3% 0-shot CoT	85.7% 0-shot CoT	88.7% 0-shot CoT	—	—
Code HumanEval	92.0% 0-shot	84.9% 0-shot	90.2% 0-shot	84.1% 0-shot	84.1% 0-shot

There are numerous additional benchmarks we could examine, but you likely grasp the general idea of how Claude 3.5 excels in many of these parameters.

Note: It's important to approach benchmarks published by model developers with caution, as they may be subject to bias.

Beyond benchmark performance, Claude 3.5 demonstrates impressive capabilities in vision tasks, allowing users to upload and analyze images. Additionally, it can generate code that users can interact with directly in the browser through a new feature called Artifacts. We will explore these features and more in depth as we progress through the book.

Chapter 2: Claude UI, Applications and Features

If you've used AI tools like Gemini, ChatGPT, Perplexity, or similar platforms, you'll find the Claude UI familiar and user-friendly. You interact with the model by typing your input:

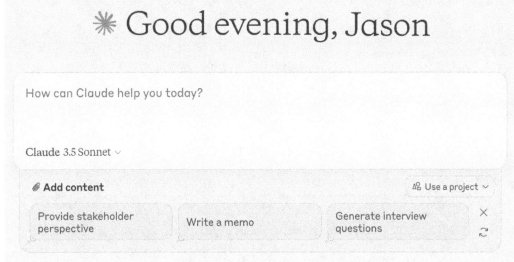

The interface also provides several placeholders to help you get started. Examples include "Write a memo" and "Generate interview questions".

After initiating a conversation, you'll be able to view your recent chats:

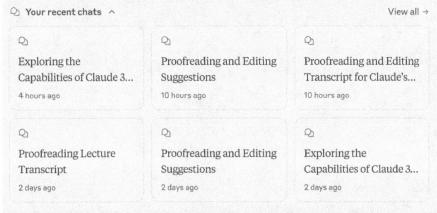

You can click "View All →" to find all your chats:

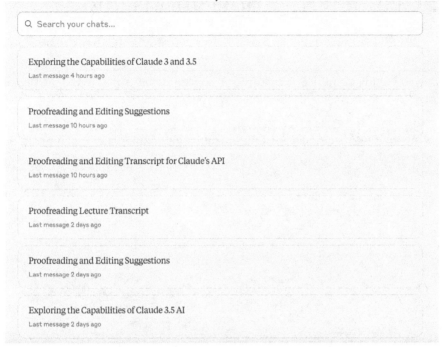

You can also find your recent chats by hovering on the left side:

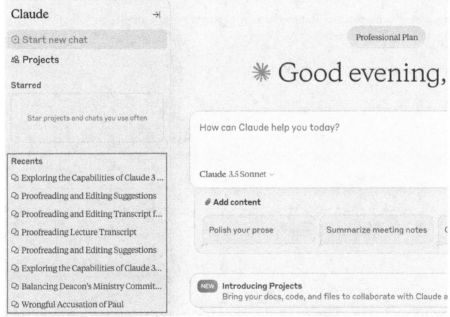

In the left sidebar, you'll find your chats, projects, and starred conversations or projects. You can save important chats by starring them, which will then appear in this sidebar for easy access.

To keep the sidebar visible at all times, you can click the "Pin Sidebar" option:

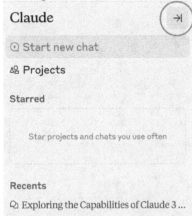

Pinning the sidebar makes it easier to access your saved items as needed. If you frequently use certain starred projects or chats, pinning the sidebar can be beneficial. However, if you prefer a simpler UI, you can leave it unpinned.

Now that we have a high-level understanding of the UI, let's start interacting with Claude:

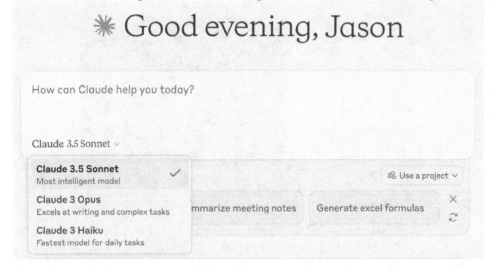

As mentioned earlier, you can select the model you want to interact with from the following options: Claude 3.5 Sonnet, Claude 3 Opus, and Claude 3 Haiku:

To access advanced features like Artifacts, you first need to enable them by navigating to 'Feature Preview':

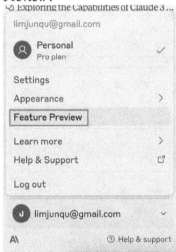

Under Artifacts, toggle 'On'.

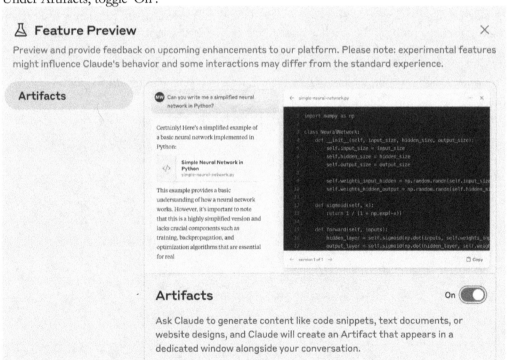

When enabled, the lab icon will be shown in the UI:

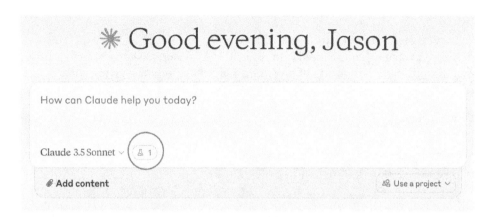

The Artifacts feature will be discussed in detail later.

How to Use Claude 3.5 Sonnet as a Writing Partner

I spend a considerable amount of time on Twitter (feel free to follow me at x.com/greglim81). It's common for people to share posts on these platforms with the assistance of a content creator. However, not everyone has the time or resources to hire a professional content creator. This is where large language models (LLMs) like Claude 3.5 can be particularly helpful.

For example, we can use Claude 3.5 Sonnet to generate posts for Twitter:

 Write a super-informative, controversial but true post about "making money" that can go viral on Twitter

Here's a provocative but factual tweet thread about making money that could potentially go viral:

1/7 Hard truth: Most "passive income" schemes are BS. Real wealth rarely comes easy. The path to riches? Solve big problems, create massive value, or exploit unfair advantages.

2/7 Wage growth is stagnant. Meanwhile, the ultra-wealthy's fortunes explode. Why? They own assets - especially equity. Your job won't make you rich. Owning pieces of valuable businesses might.

3/7 "Follow your passion" is feel-good garbage for most. Follow market demand instead. Your dream job probably won't make you wealthy. But filling an urgent need people will pay for? That's the ticket.

4/7 Formal education is often overrated for wealth-building. Many of the richest are college dropouts. What matters more? Developing rare & valuable skills, building networks, and gaining real-world experience.

19

Claude 3.5 Sonnet can create highly informative posts that are ready to share. You can apply this method to your own niche, leveraging your expertise to refine the AI-generated content before posting. This approach can significantly ease the process of growing your online presence, giving you a competitive edge.

You can easily adapt this technique for LinkedIn posts by slightly modifying the prompt:

 Write a super-informative, controversial but true post about
"making money" that can go viral on LinkedIn

Instead of starting from scratch, Claude provides you with a solid foundation to build upon. However, it's crucial to remember that you should always incorporate your personal insights and expertise into the final content. Avoid posting AI-generated content without modifications, as this can lead to potential issues.

After the response is generated, you have the option to either copy it directly or request a new generation.

If you choose to retry, Claude will display both responses (labeled as 1/2 and 2/2), allowing you to select the most suitable option.

Copy Retry ‹ 2/2 › 👍 👎

You can provide feedback to the model by rating responses as positive (thumbs up) or negative (thumbs down). This feedback mechanism helps refine the model's future responses to better align with your preferences.

If you're not satisfied with a response, you can modify your prompt with additional details to guide the output. For example, you could enhance your prompt by specifying:
"Make this post 1500 words, use proper MDX formatting, and incorporate the keyword phrase 'Future of Making Money' throughout."

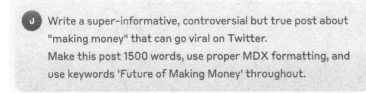 Write a super-informative, controversial but true post about
"making money" that can go viral on Twitter.
Make this post 1500 words, use proper MDX formatting, and
use keywords 'Future of Making Money' throughout.

This detailed prompt will guide the model to incorporate these specific requirements, resulting in a more tailored and suitable response.

As the response is generated, you'll notice that it includes various structural and formatting elements such as headings, subheadings, MDX formatting, image placeholders, and other formatting details:

←   The Future of Making Money: Controversial Truths   ✕

The Future of Making Money: Uncomfortable Truths for the Digital Age

In an era of rapid technological advancement and economic shifts, the future of making money is evolving faster than ever before. This post delves into some controversial yet factual perspectives on wealth creation in the modern world. Buckle up – some of these insights might challenge your long-held beliefs about financial success.

1. The Death of the Traditional Career Path

The idea of climbing the corporate ladder to financial stability is becoming increasingly obsolete. In the future of making money, loyalty to a single company for decades is more likely to leave you financially vulnerable than secure.

Why this matters:

- Job security is an illusion in the age of AI and automation
- Skill obsolescence happens at an accelerating rate
- Pension plans and long-term benefits are disappearing

Chapter 3: Claude Artifacts

Artifacts is a new feature of Claude 3.5 Sonnet that provides a dynamic screen for displaying various types of output. This includes:
- executable code snippets
- images
- text documents
- website designs
- and more

This feature allows you to view and edit the output while maintaining an ongoing conversation with Claude 3.5 Sonnet.

To access the Artifacts feature, navigate to settings and select "Feature Preview":

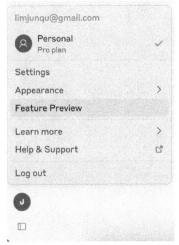

Enable it:

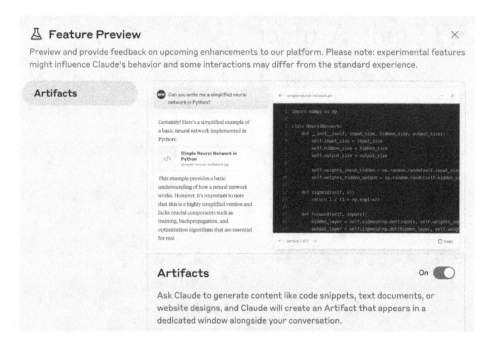

Once you have Artifacts enabled, close the pop-up, and you'll see a lab icon indicating that one experimental feature is enabled:

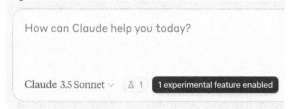

Currently, Artifacts is an experimental feature. This allows Claude to gather user feedback before implementing it for all users. When activated, the feature creates an artifact that appears in a dedicated window alongside your conversation.

Artifacts generate code or documents separately to keep the UI clean. If your code requires no external libraries, Claude can actually run that code in the UI for you, which is very useful. Let's explore an example. We'll use the following prompt:

"Can you write a piece of code for plotting the population from the 1900s to 2020 and make it interactive without installing external libraries?"

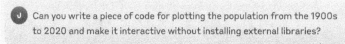

Claude will start writing the code. You can see the code in its entirety when you click on the code tab:

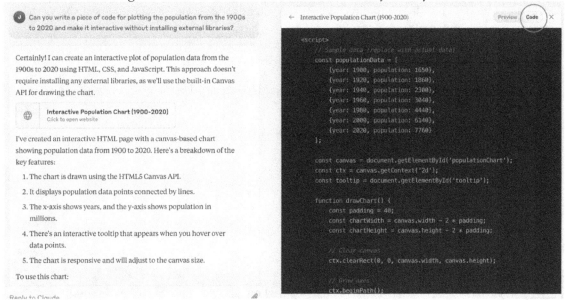

Preview tab:

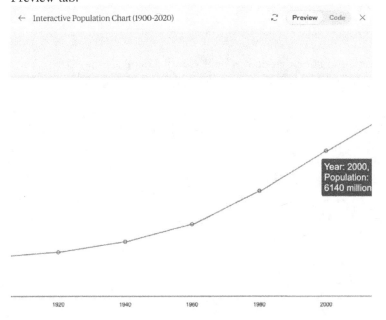

And it not only generates code, the preview of the code is also interactive. For example, it shows the world population was 6,140 million in 2020, and as you hover over other year points, it shows the different population figures interactively.

You can make changes in real time. For instance, we could say, "Can you present this in a bar graph?":

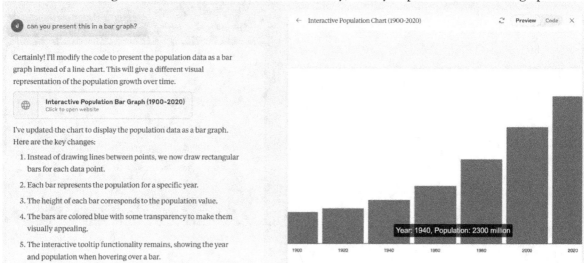

So you can present data in multiple formats e.g. line chart, bar graph, pie chart etc.

Note that currently, the model can only run code that do not have external dependencies. If you're building something that requires importing an external package, it won't be able to run it.

You can also upload data to Artifacts. For example, I downloaded a dataset of 2023-2024 NBA Player Stats from Kaggle (https://www.kaggle.com/datasets/mohamedsaqibshouqi/2023-2024-nba-player-stats-playoffs):

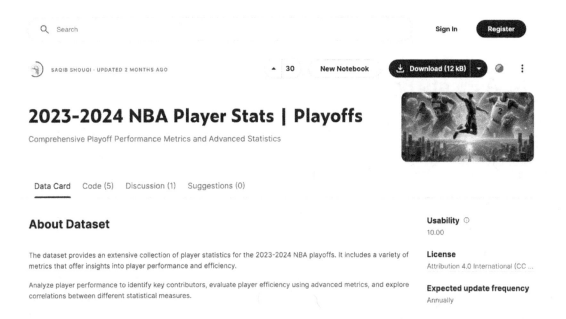

Click on 'Download' to download the dataset in .csv format. I then upload the .csv file into Claude:

And give it a prompt like:

"Create a dashboard which lets me change model parameters to predict each NBA player's points. Use just HTML and CSS"

And I will get a dashboard to adjust parameters to predict points of NBA players:

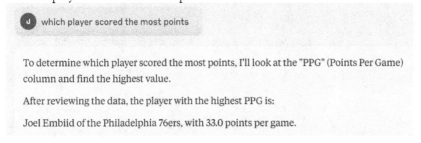

So you can see how Artifacts creates a dynamic workspace where users can see, edit and build on Claude's creations in real time.

Analyzing Data

You can also ask data analysis questions about datasets you have uploaded. For example, you can ask: "Which player scored the most points?"

> **J** which player scored the most points
>
> To determine which player scored the most points, I'll look at the "PPG" (Points Per Game) column and find the highest value.
>
> After reviewing the data, the player with the highest PPG is:
>
> Joel Embiid of the Philadelphia 76ers, with 33.0 points per game.

Or: "Give me a bar graph of how many points each player scored"

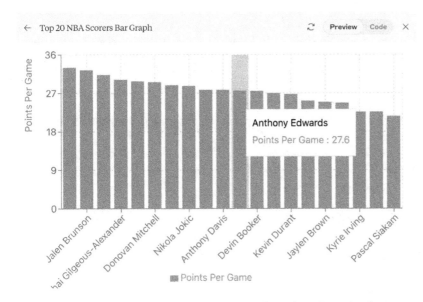

This is how we can provide datasets to Claude and analyze the data.

Creating Games

We can also ask Claude to help create games. Let's prompt Claude:
"create a fully working snake game web app with scoring system"

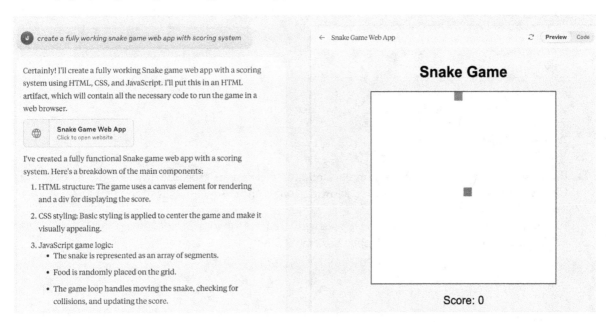

In my case surprisingly, it only took one attempt to build a fully working snake game with a scoring system. You can render the game on the Artifacts canvas and play the game!

You can take this further by adding more complex features like stages, lives, etc.

However, some games do not work the first time. You may need to redo the prompt or add more specific instructions on how the game should work.

Creating a Calculator App

Let's next try creating a working calculator web app with this prompt:
"Create a simple calculator web application"

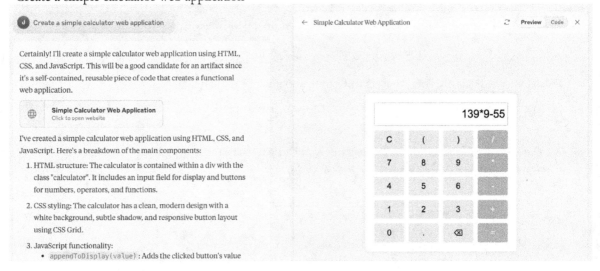

You can test out the calculator live in the Artifacts canvas.

Building Websites

Building a website from scratch is complex and time-consuming, especially if you're not a developer. Claude Artifacts simplifies this process, allowing you to create functional websites with ease.

Prompt: "Create a personal portfolio website with sections for an 'About Me' page, a 'Projects' gallery, a 'Blog' for sharing articles, and a 'Contact' form."

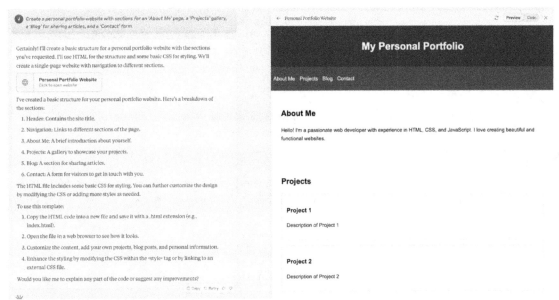

Creating Diagrams and Flowcharts

Another awesome feature of Artifacts is its ability to create diagrams and flowcharts. In the example below, I asked Claude to create a graphical illustration of Retrieval Augmented Generation (RAGs) (file from Microsoft's RAG in Azure AI Search: learn.microsoft.com/en-us/azure/search/retrieval-augmented-generation-overview)

Prompt: "Create a graphical overview of RAGs"

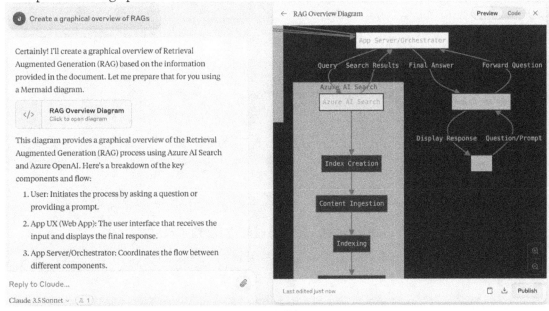

Pretty cool, right? You can download these files and open them locally with another program, allowing for further customization and integration into presentations or reports.

Presentation Deck

Professionals and educators can create a compelling presentation deck in a matter of seconds with Claude Artifacts. I uploaded the Nestle Company annual report (https://www.nestle.com/sites/default/files/2024-02/2023-annual-review-en.pdf) and give it the following prompt:
"Create a presentation deck, including slides for the company overview, market analysis, product features, business model, and financial projections. The presentation should have multiple slides that user can switch to next and previous slides by clicking the arrow keys."

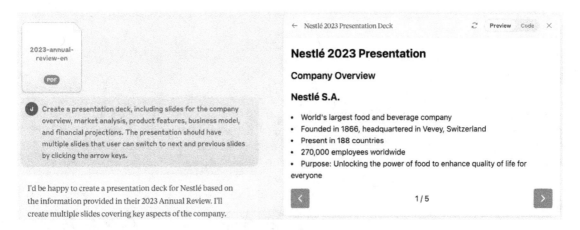

Data Analysis

Let's look at a last example. I downloaded a World Population dataset from Kaggle.

After uploading this to Claude, I asked it to "help me visualize this document in a line chart. Create an HTML page using the data. Make it interactive."

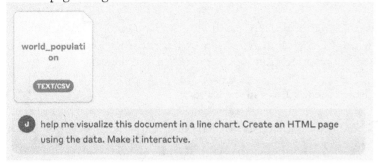

This demonstrates how you can take a document from the web with data points and create visualizations.

In this case, the world population dataset is quite large, so Claude might not be able to process it all at once due to context window limitations. It did manage to write some code and create a partial preview, but it couldn't render all the values in one go.

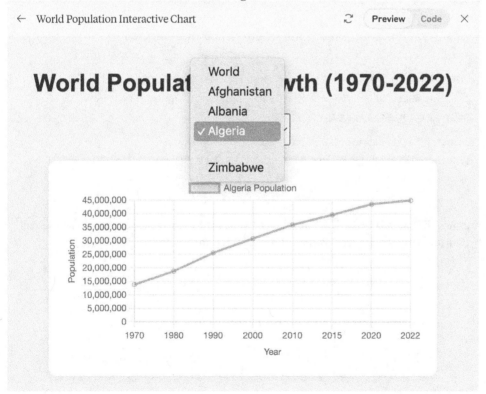

In our case, it only shows the data for partial countries, i.e. Afghanistan, Albania, Algeria and Zimbabwe.

Typically, you wouldn't have a dataset as large as world population by each country. You'd usually have around 100-200 items to visualize, which Claude can handle more easily. The ideal approach would be to ask Claude to write the code, which you can then run separately to visualize the data.

For smaller datasets, Claude can directly visualize them in the artifact.

You can also ask Claude questions about the data, such as "Which country has the highest population?"

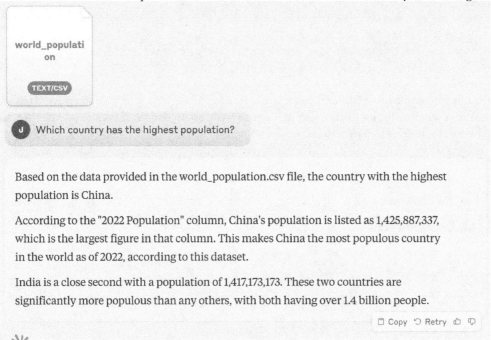

or "Which country has the highest growth from the start year to the most recent year?" Claude will analyze the CSV data and provide answers based on its calculations.

J Which country has the highest growth from the start year to the most recent year?

To determine which country has the highest growth from the start year to the most recent year, I'll need to compare the earliest population data (1970) with the most recent (2022) for each country. This will involve calculating the percentage growth for each country and finding the highest.

However, doing this calculation for all 234 countries would be time-consuming and prone to errors if done manually. Instead, I can identify a few countries with notably high growth rates and compare them.

Looking at the "Growth Rate" column, which likely represents recent annual growth, some of the highest values are:

1. Niger: 1.0378

2. Angola: 1.0315

3. Uganda: 1.0304

4. Mali: 1.0314

5. Chad: 1.0316

Let's calculate the growth for these countries from 1970 to 2022:

These are the typical use cases you'd want to solve with Claude's upload feature. Be aware of the context window limit when inputting large amounts of data. However, if you're working with basic code (like HTML) and connecting it with your CSVs, it shouldn't be a problem in most cases.

This concludes our overview of the Artifact feature. It's a powerful tool, and I hope I've given you a high-level understanding of how it works.

Chapter 4: Introduction to Claude Projects

Claude has a feature called 'Projects' where you can feed a 'Project' specific instructions, incorporate additional knowledge through documents, and then chat with it to enable idea generation, more strategic decision-making, and better results.

You can save this 'Project' without inputting the same specific instructions/docuyments the next time you want to use it.

Each project has a 200k context window, equivalent of a 500 page book, for users to add relevant documents, code and insights to enchance Claude's effectiveness.

For example, you can create a Claude Project to help you plan your meals and another for analyzing legal documents—two different use cases, two different custom Projects:

Healthy Meal Project

Legal Project

It is similar to ChatGPT's Custom GPT.

Note: 'Projects' are available only for Pro or Team users.

Once you have a Pro or Team account, to create a Project, in your Claude dashboard, go to "Projects" (menu item on the left)

Here, you should see your "Projects", and the ability to create a Project at the top-right. Click on 'Create Project':

For instance, I want to create a Project that helps me create healthy diets for weight loss. I can input "I want to build a Project to help me generate healthy diets for weight loss."

After 'Create Project', in the next screen, go to 'Set custom instructions':

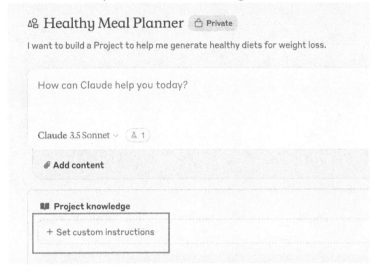

And I can provide custom instructions e.g. "I want to build a Project to help me generate healthy diets for weight loss." I can add in a constraint that "I am allergic to eggs.":

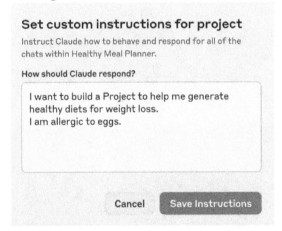

Click on 'Save Instructions' and the Project knowledge will include our custom instructions:

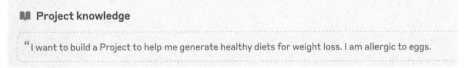

We can interact with our Project by giving it a prompt like "What's a good weight-loss lunch idea?":

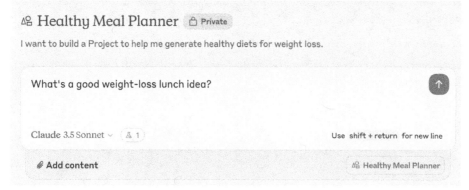

Claude will proceed to suggest lunch ideas and take into consideration that I am allergic to eggs.

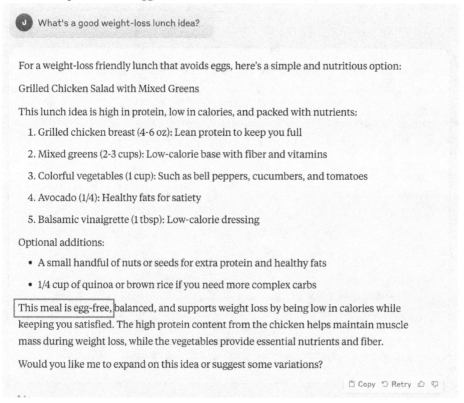

Your Project will now be saved and you can access it under the 'Projects' page.

If you 'star' your project, you can access your project under 'Starred' on the left pane:

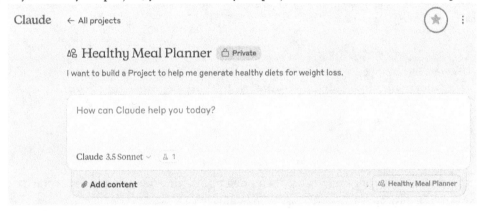

Editing your Project

It is very unlikely that you will create a useful Claude Project just by typing a few instructions. However, the good news is that you can easily edit the Project and make it more useful as you use it. For instance, you may notice something you don't like about the Project and want to edit it.

To edit the Project knowledge, simply select "Edit":

For example, if you want tomatoes in every meal, and also include an estimate of the number of calories in the meal, we append this to the instruction:

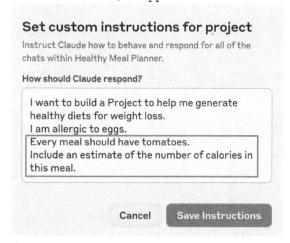

The Project will update to reflect your preference, attempting to include tomatoes and the estimated calories in every meal. So if I prompt it again "Suggest a breakfast":

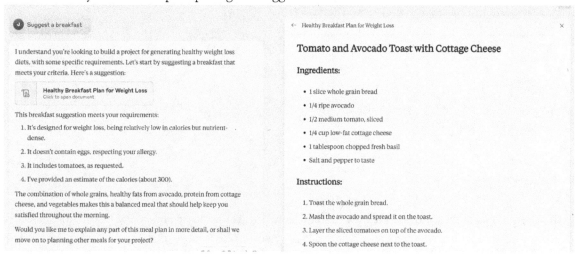

Nutritional Information:

- Estimated total calories: ~300 calories
- Protein: ~15g
- Carbohydrates: ~30g
- Healthy fats: ~15g

You can now see it includes tomatoes and the approximate calories of the meal.

Providing Structured Instructions

When providing instructions, structuring them can be beneficial. For instance, if you want to specify preferred ingredients, you could start a new section titled "Ingredients I Prefer" and list them in bullet points or a structured format, like chicken breast, avocados, and lettuce:

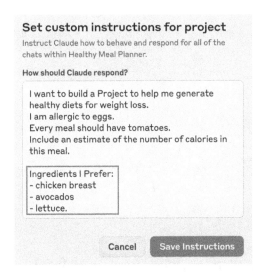

This structured approach not only makes it easier to add or remove items but also helps the Project to identify key information more efficiently.

You might also include a list of ingredients that should be suggested less frequently. This approach provides more context and tailors the Project to your needs. For instance, you can mention, "The following ingredients are okay but should not be suggested often," followed by a list like olive, beef, and eggplant:

Once you have edited the instructions to your satisfaction, select 'Save Instructions'. Let's now try a sample prompt "Recommend me a healthy snack":

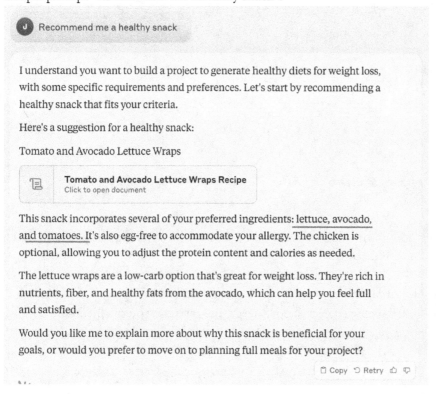

You can see that it includes preferred ingredients like avocado, lettuce, tomatoes, and avoids ingredients not to be suggested often.

You can go back to the instructions and ask for more precise information, like including calorie count for each ingredient. We can specify this in the instructions:

How should Claude respond?

healthy diets for weight loss.
I am allergic to eggs.
Every meal should have tomatoes.
Include an estimate of the number of calories in this meal.

Ingredients I Prefer:
- chicken breast
- avocados
- lettuce.

include the calories count for each ingredient

And if we prompt the Project again, we get:

← Healthy Meal Plan for Weight Loss

Healthy Meal Plan for Weight Loss

Breakfast

- Grilled chicken breast (3 oz): 165 calories
- Avocado (1/4): 80 calories
- Cherry tomatoes (1/2 cup): 15 calories
- Lettuce (1 cup): 5 calories

Total calories: 265

Lunch

- Chicken and avocado salad:
  - Grilled chicken breast (4 oz): 220 calories
  - Avocado (1/2): 160 calories
  - Cherry tomatoes (1 cup): 30 calories
  - Lettuce (2 cups): 10 calories
  - Olive oil dressing (1 tbsp): 120 calories

The aim is to be as explicit as possible in your instructions, leaving little room for interpretation. If the Project exhibits undesirable behavior, refine the instructions to clarify what is acceptable and what is not. For e.g., you can also specify the presentation of the response:

How should Claude respond?

- lettuce.

The following ingredients are okay but should not be suggested often:
- olive
- beef
- eggplant

include the calories count for each ingredient

Have the ingredients in a table, not a list bullet point format

Response:

← Healthy Weight Loss Meal Plan   ✕

Healthy Weight Loss Meal Plan

Breakfast (Approximately 400 calories)

Ingredient	Amount	Calories
Chicken Breast	100g	165
Avocado	1/2 medium	160
Tomatoes	1 medium	22
Lettuce	1 cup, shredded	5
Whole Grain Toast	1 slice	70

Total Calories: 422

Recipe: Grill the chicken breast and slice it. Serve on top of a bed of lettuce and sliced tomatoes. Add sliced avocado on the side and a piece of whole grain toast.

Lunch (Approximately 450 calories)

Ingredient	Amount	Calories
Chicken Breast	120g	198
Avocado	1/4 medium	80

Also, if you want a desired structure in the response like "Overview, Prep Time, Ingredients, Instructions," specify this in the instructions.

How should Claude respond?

- eggplant

include the calories count for each ingredient

Have the ingredients in a table, not a list bullet point format

The response should have the following structure:
- Summary: Quick Summary of the meal plan
- Ingredients
- Instructions

And you get something like:

Healthy Weight Loss Meal Plan

Summary

This meal plan features a balanced, low-calorie dinner centered around chicken breast, with a focus on incorporating tomatoes and your preferred ingredients. The meal is egg-free to accommodate your allergy. A healthy snack option is also included.

Dinner: Grilled Chicken Salad with Avocado and Tomatoes

Ingredients

Ingredient	Amount	Calories
Chicken breast	150g	165
Avocado	1/2	160
Lettuce	2 cups	10
Tomatoes	1 medium	22
Olive oil	1 tsp	40
Lemon juice	1 tbsp	4
Salt and pepper	To taste	0

Total calories: Approximately 401

Instructions

1. Season the chicken breast with salt and pepper.
2. Grill the chicken breast until fully cooked (internal temperature of 165°F or 74°C)

In summary, controlling the output from Claude Projects involves detailed, specific instructions and a structured approach, allowing for customization in a specific format according to your needs and preferences.

And the good thing is, the next time someone wants to query the Healthy AI planner, they don't have to input all the custom instructions all over again in a new chat. With Projects, you can get started much faster.

Other use cases of Projects to automate daily tasks include when you write a novel. The success of the novel depends on its consistency, e.g., the names of the characters, their backstory, and these can be specified in the initial data you feed to the knowledge base.

Or say you work on the latest new programming language that Claude does not yet have access to. You can upload the documentation of the new language to the Project, and have it generate code which is more aligned to the new programming language's style and format.

Chapter 5: Enchancing Instructions for Project Performance

In this chapter, we continue learning techniques to improve the instructions we provide to our Project. This time, we'll create a new Project from scratch to understand a different use case.

I aim to create a Project that guides you on self publishing books on Amazon. Fun fact: I've published over twenty books on Amazon (including this one), sold over 60,000 copies and earned over $200,000 in royalties. So its something I really enjoy!

Let's assume we're developing this Project to help beginners author their first book. Now, there's a lot of generic publishing information, but I will provide the information which I thing is most crucial and which I have my own experiences..

We'll start with something basic to provide context and kickstart the Project's creation:

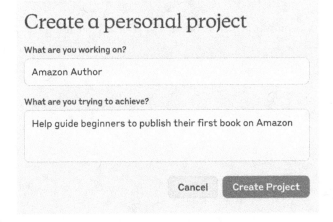

Let's prompt it: "What tool should I use to create my book manuscript? " will be the first prompt offered:

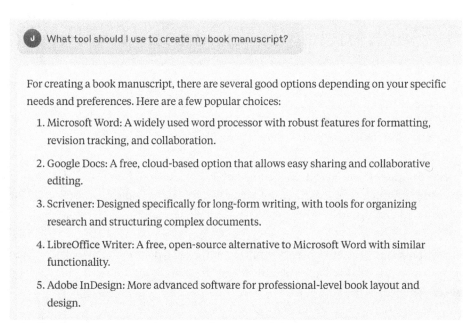

Initially, the Project provides a list of generic information about tools used to create a manuscript.

But I can add the specific tool I feel is best for a beginner, which is Microsoft Word. Try setting the below custom instructions:

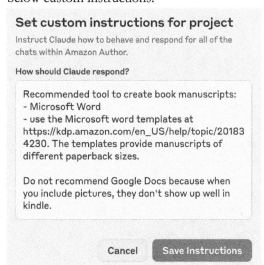

I provided additional information on where you can download ready made MS Word templates for various paperback sizes.

After updating the instructions, I'll test the prompt again, "What tool should I use to create my book manuscript?" to see if the new instructions are considered. And I get:

 What tool should I use to create my book manuscript?

Based on your requirements, I recommend using Microsoft Word to create your book manuscript. Here's why:

1. Microsoft Word is a robust word processing tool widely used for creating book manuscripts.

2. It offers better compatibility with the publishing industry standards.

3. As you mentioned, Amazon KDP (Kindle Direct Publishing) provides Microsoft Word templates for different paperback sizes. These templates are specifically designed to work well with their publishing system.

4. Word handles images better for Kindle formatting, which is crucial since you noted that pictures don't show up well when using Google Docs.

5. Word offers advanced formatting options that can be helpful for book layout, such as styles, headers, footers, and page numbering.

To get started:

1. Download the appropriate Microsoft Word template from the Amazon KDP website (https://kdp.amazon.com/en_US/help/topic/201834230) based on your desired paperback size.

2. Use this template as a base for your manuscript, which will help ensure your book meets Amazon's formatting requirements.

As per my instructions, the Project recommends MS-Word and provides the link to the templates.

We also further personalize constraints for the Project for e.g.: if a user asks if they should use Google Docs for manuscripts. The Project replies as per our instructions:

 do you recommend Google docs to create manuscripts?

No, I do not recommend using Google Docs to create manuscripts, especially if you plan to include pictures in your book. There are a few key reasons for this:

1. Image handling: As you mentioned, pictures don't show up well when transferring from Google Docs to Kindle formats. This can significantly impact the quality and appearance of your final book.

I can further specify to add in the footnote that, if the user wants to find out more information about book publishing, they can visit greglim.gumroad.com:

How should Claude respond?

- use the Microsoft word templates at https://kdp.amazon.com/en_US/help/topic/20183 4230. The templates provide manuscripts of different paperback sizes.

Do not recommend Google Docs because when you include pictures, they don't show up well in kindle.

In all responses, add that if the user wants to find out more information about book publishing, they can visit greglim.gumroad.com

Testing these instructions, we now see that the Project directs users to greglim.gumroad.com if they want more information.

 what tool to use to create manuscripts

Based on your requirements, I recommend using Microsoft Word to create book manuscripts. Here's why:

1. Microsoft Word is a widely used and feature-rich word processing software that offers excellent formatting and layout options for book manuscripts.

2. Amazon KDP (Kindle Direct Publishing) provides specific Microsoft Word templates for different paperback sizes, which you can download from https://kdp.amazon.com/en_US/help/topic/201834230. These templates are designed to ensure your manuscript meets the formatting requirements for various book sizes, making the publishing process smoother.

3. Microsoft Word handles images well, which is crucial for maintaining picture quality when publishing on Kindle. This is an advantage over Google Docs, which you mentioned can have issues with image display on Kindle.

4. Word offers advanced features like styles, headers, footers, and page numbering, which are essential for professional manuscript formatting.

5. It's compatible with most publishing platforms and can easily export to PDF format if needed.

If you want to find out more information about book publishing, you can visit greglim.gumroad.com.

To excel at prompt engineering, learn more at Claude's site:
https://docs.anthropic.com/en/docs/build-with-claude/prompt-engineering/overview

It contains guidance on writing effective instructions that guide the Project to produce desired responses. Essentially, detailed instructions yield more accurate responses.

Claude Projects are only available privately as of this book's writing, but I believe it will soon be possible to share Projects with other users and customers:

A⚬ Amazon Author 🔒 Private

More Specific Instructions

Lastly, let's make our Project more comprehensive by specifying marketing strategies that I've found best for selling books on Amazon. Add the below instructions:

> **How should Claude respond?**
>
> In all responses, add that if the user wants to find out more information about book publishing, they can visit greglim.gumroad.com
>
> Best book marketing strategies:
> - have as many five star reviews as possible for your book
> - make your book available in as many formats as possible, e.g. kindle, paperback, hardcopy, audio
> - have important keywords in your book title
> - have an attractive book cover

And if you prompt the Project, it responses with:

J what marketing strategies work best for amazon books

Based on the information provided and general best practices for marketing Amazon books, here are some effective strategies:

1. Optimize your book listing:
   - Include important keywords in your book title and subtitle
   - Create an attractive book cover that stands out in search results
   - Write a compelling book description that hooks potential readers

2. Maximize book formats:
   - Make your book available in as many formats as possible (e.g., Kindle, paperback, hardcover, audiobook)
   - This increases visibility and caters to different reader preferences

3. Gather positive reviews:
   - Aim to accumulate as many five-star reviews as possible
   - Consider offering advance reader copies (ARCs) to get early reviews
   - Encourage satisfied readers to leave reviews

4. Utilize Amazon's promotional tools:
   - Set up Amazon Author Central to manage your author profile
   - Use Amazon's free promotion days (if enrolled in KDP Select)
   - Consider running price promotions or Countdown Deals

You can see that it uses my own personalized instructions, plus existing generic information about book publishing.

Working with Documents

Try applying what you have learned in this chapter to create your own Claude Projects! For e.g. you can have a Project for a restaurant with the menu instructions:

Below are the details for my restaurant:

Name: Wild West Grille
Address: 452 Prairie Lane, Boulder, CO 80301
Phone: (303) 555-0192

Appetizers:
Buffalo Wings - $8.99: Classic spicy wings served with blue cheese dressing.
Loaded Potato Skins - $7.50: Crispy potato skins filled with cheese, bacon, and green onions.
Texas Nachos - $9.50: Tortilla chips piled high with beef chili, jalapenos, cheese, and sour cream.

Entrees:
BBQ Ribs Full Rack - $22.99: Slow-cooked ribs with a smoky BBQ sauce served with fries and coleslaw.
Grilled Salmon - $18.50: Fresh salmon fillet with a lemon butter sauce, served with rice and vegetables.
Chicken Alfredo Pasta - $15.99: Grilled chicken breast over fettuccine pasta in a creamy Alfredo sauce.
New York Strip Steak - $24.99: 12 oz. strip steak grilled to order with mashed potatoes and seasonal vegetables.

Burgers & Sandwiches:
Classic Cheeseburger - $12.99: A juicy beef patty with lettuce, tomato, onion, and cheese on a brioche bun.
BBQ Pulled Pork Sandwich - $13.50: Tender pulled pork in BBQ sauce on a toasted bun with coleslaw.
Veggie Burger - $11.99: A delicious plant-based patty with avocado and sprouts on a wheat bun.

Salads:
Caesar Salad - $10.99: Add Chicken $3.50: Romaine lettuce with croutons, parmesan cheese, and Caesar dressing.
Southwest Chicken Salad - $14.99: Grilled chicken with mixed greens, corn, black beans, cheese, and ranch dressing.

Because the manu instructions are very long, I can put the instructions in a Word doc and upload them by clicking on 'Add Content':

Claude will also reflect the percentage knowledge size used .

And I can query it:

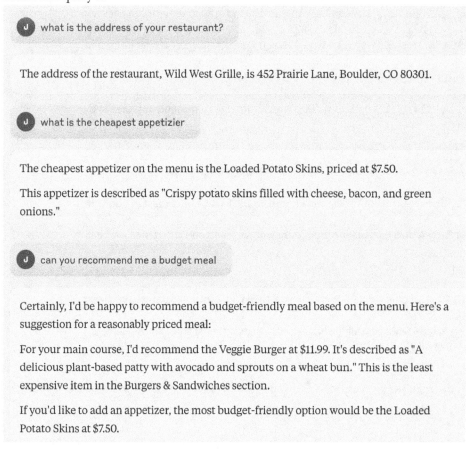

You will get customized responses based on the document you have uploaded. Claude allows you the option to add custom instructions via text and also upload documents like .doc, pdf, and many more.

Claude will then reference these documents in its conversations.

For example, you can copy and paste entire text content from websites and upload it into a Project, then ask Claude to create a blog post.

Or you can upload writing style best practices and have Claude provide expert assistance, such as writing emails like your marketing team.

I look forward to your own Claude Project inventions!

Chapter 6: Introduction to Claude API

In this chapter, we are going to walk through how to use the Claude API. If you are not familiar with the concept of APIs, it's likely you are not a developer, and this section may not be relevant for you. But it will still be useful to stay around and learn how APIs work and how you can use the Claude API to potentially make apps that earn you some money.

So far, we have been using Claude from its website. But you can create your own custom apps, for example, chat bots that connect to Claude 3.5 in the backend.

In this chapter, we explore creating a handwriting analysis app using Claude 3.5 Sonnet's advanced vision capabilities. We'll build a powerful web application with Streamlit that lets you upload images of handwriting and receive insightful personality interpretations.

I will be using Visual Studio Code as my code editor (code.visualstudio.com). You can use your own preferred code editor.

If you have not installed python, you can download and install it from python.org/downloads/.

Getting Started

We start by creating a virtual environment and activating it to keep dependencies cleanly separated from other app projects. In the Terminal, run:

```
python -m venv venv
source venv/bin/activate
```

```
(base) MacBook-Air-4:claude user$ python -m venv venv
(base) MacBook-Air-4:claude user$ source venv/bin/activate
(venv) (base) MacBook-Air-4:claude user$ ▌
```

Then we install Anthropic with *pip*:

```
pip install anthropic
```

We create a new file named *app.py* in Visual Studio Code.

Fill *app.py* with the following code:

```python
import anthropic

client = anthropic.Anthropic()

message = client.messages.create(
    model="claude-3-5-sonnet-20240620",
    max_tokens=1000,
    messages=[
        {
            "role": "user",
            "content": [
                {
                    "type": "text",
                    "text": "Hi"
                }
            ]
        }
    ]
)

print(message.content)
```

Note: If you prefer to copy and paste, contact support@i-ducate.com for the source code

Code Explanation

```
import anthropic

client = anthropic.Anthropic()
```

We first import Anthropic, then create a client to interact with the Anthropic API.

```
message = client.messages.create(
    model="claude-3-5-sonnet-20240620",
    max_tokens=1000,
```

For this, we call *client.messages.create*, and pass the model "claude-3-5-sonnet-20240620" as a parameter. We set the maximum number of tokens to 1000.

```
    messages=[
        {
            "role": "user",
            "content": [
                {
                    "type": "text",
                    "text": "Hi"
                }
            ]
        }
    ]
```

We define the messages to send to the model, starting with the "user" role. We send a simple text message "Hi".

```
print(message.content)
```

We print the result of this call to the console.

Anthropic API key

Before we run our app, we need to set up an Anthropic API key. Go to the Anthropic website (https://www.anthropic.com), and in the navigation bar under 'Claude', click on 'API'.

Select 'Start Building':

Log in, and you will be brought to the dashboard. Select 'Get API keys'.

Click on 'Create Key':

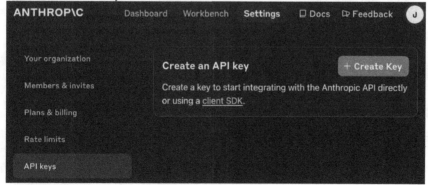

Give the key a name:

Copy the key:

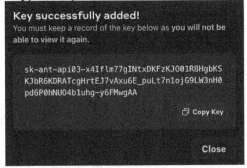

and paste it in the terminal with the command:

```
export ANTHROPIC_API_KEY=<insert your own key here>
```

For e.g., it will look something like:

```
(venv) (base) MacBook-Air-4:claude user$ export ANTHROPIC_API_KEY=sk-ant-api03-x4Iflm77gINtxDKFzKJO01R8HgbKSKJbR6KDRATcgHrtEJ7vAxu
6E_puLt7n1ojG9LW3nH0pd6P0hNUO4b1uhg-y6FMwgAA
```

Before we start our script, back in the Claude dashboard, you should be able to claim $5 worth of free credits for testing:

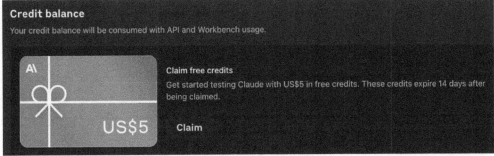

Or if the offer doesn't exist, you can sign up with an initial $5 to test things out.

Now we can start the script with
`python app.py`

We should get a message back from the model:
```
(venv) (base) MacBook-Air-4:claude user$ python app.py
[TextBlock(text='Hello! How can I assist you today? Feel free to ask me any ques
tions or let me know if you need help with anything.', type='text')]
(venv) (base) MacBook-Air-4:claude user$
```

Congratulations! That's means we have successfully connected to the Claude API.

Analyzing an Image

Next, we want to actually analyze an image. We will take this nice picture here of the Eiffel tower and convert it to base 64.

In *app.py*, add in the lines in **bold**:

```
import anthropic
import base64
import httpx

client = anthropic.Anthropic()

image_url="https://upload.wikimedia.org/wikipedia/commons/thumb/8/85/Tour
  Eiffel Wikimedia Commons %28cropped%29.jpg/800px-
Tour Eiffel Wikimedia Commons %28cropped%29.jpg"
```

```
image_data = base64.b64encode(httpx.get(image_url).content).decode("utf-
8")
```

```
message = client.messages.create(
...

...
```

We fetch an image from a given URL using the HTTPX library, encode the image content to base 64, and then decodes it into a UTF 8 string.

This string is then sent to the Anthropic API for analysis. We then add in **bold**:

```
message = client.messages.create(
    model="claude-3-5-sonnet-20240620",
    max_tokens=1000,
    messages=[
        {
            "role": "user",
            "content": [
                {
                    "type": "image",
                    "source": {
                        "type": "base64",
                        "media_type": "image/jpeg",
                        "data": image_data
                    }
                },
                {
                    "type": "text",
                    "text": "Describe the image",
                }
            ]
        }
    ]
)
```

Code Explanation

```
                {
                    "type": "image",
                    "source": {
                        "type": "base64",
                        "media_type": "image/jpeg",
                        "data": image_data
                    }
                },
```

We specify the type as image, and pass the following parameters under source type as *base64*, media type as image/jpeg and data as the base64 encoded string.

```
        },
        {
            "type": "text",
            "text": "Describe the image",
        }
```

We change the prompt to "Describe the image". Now, let's run the script with:

```
python app.py
```

We see that the image is correctly analyzed and it's impressive how detailed the description is:

```
(venv) (base) MacBook-Air-4:claude user$ python app.py
[TextBlock(text="This image showcases the iconic Eiffel Tower in Paris, France. The tower is captured in i
ts full height against a clear blue sky, demonstrating its impressive iron lattice structure. The view is
from ground level, allowing the viewer to appreciate the tower's grand scale and intricate design.\n\nAt t
he base of the tower, you can see the wide arches that form its foundation. The tower tapers as it rises,
with multiple levels visible, including observation decks. At the very top, there's a spire and what appea
rs to be communications equipment.\n\nIn the foreground, there's a large grassy area known as the Champ de
 Mars, which serves as a public park. Trees line the edges of this green space, and you can see small figu
res of people enjoying the area, giving a sense of scale to the massive structure.\n\nIn the background, b
eyond the tower, you can see some buildings that appear to be part of the Trocadéro, which faces the Eiffe
l Tower from across the Seine River.\n\nThe image captures the essence of this world-famous landmark, show
casing its architectural beauty and its prominent place in the Parisian landscape.", type='text')]
(venv) (base) MacBook-Air-4:claude user$ ▮
```

However, our actual goal is not to analyze pictures in general but to analyze handwriting. For this, we change the user prompt to:

```
...
    messages=[
        {
            "role": "user",
            "content": [
                {
                ...
                },
                {
                    "type": "text",
                    "text": """Analyze handwriting by observing pressure,
size, spacing, slant, baseline, letter shapes, speed, and length. These
factors can reveal personality traits such as emotional intensity,
independence, openness, stability, and ambition.""",
                }
            ]
        }
    ]
...
```

66

As an example, we use the signature of country star Tex Williams:

We specify the image below:

```
client = anthropic.Anthropic()
```

image_url="https://upload.wikimedia.org/wikipedia/commons/e/e6/Signiture_of_country_stat%2C_Tex_Williams-_2013-04-07_11-37.jpg"
```
image_data = base64.b64encode(httpx.get(image_url).content).decode("utf-8")
...
```

Now we run *app.py*:

```
(venv) (base) MacBook-Air-4:claude user$ python app.py
[TextBlock(text="Based on the handwriting in the image, here's an analysis of some key characteristics:\n\
n1. Pressure: The signature appears to have moderate to heavy pressure, suggesting emotional intensity and
 commitment.\n\n2. Size: The writing is relatively large, which can indicate confidence and outgoing perso
nality.\n\n3. Spacing: Letters are connected, showing a fluid thought process and ability to link ideas.\n
\n4. Slant: There's a slight rightward slant, potentially indicating a balance between logic and emotion,
with a tendency towards extroversion.\n\n5. Baseline: The signature maintains a fairly straight baseline,
suggesting stability and self-control.\n\n6. Letter shapes: The writing style is quite stylized and person
alized, which could indicate creativity and individuality.\n\n7. Speed: The fluidity of the signature sugg
ests it was written fairly quickly, possibly indicating efficiency and decisiveness.\n\n8. Length: The sig
nature takes up a good amount of space, potentially showing self-assurance and comfort with attention.\n\n
Overall, this handwriting suggests a personality that is confident, expressive, and potentially creative.
The person might be outgoing and comfortable in the spotlight, with a good balance of emotional expression
 and self-control. The stylized nature of the signature could indicate someone in a creative or public-fac
ing role.\n\nIt's important to note that handwriting analysis is not a scientifically proven method of per
sonality assessment, and these interpretations should be taken as speculative rather than definitive.", ty
pe='text')]
```

And we get a detailed analysis indicating the writing is relatively large, indicating confidence and outgoing personality. It also mentions a slight rightward slant, indicating a balance between logic and emotion.

Try analyzing other handwriting images on your own!

User Interface

Now we want to build a user interface for users to upload their own images. Before we proceed, in *app.py*, we remove the hardcoding of the previous image:

```
...
client = anthropic.Anthropic()

image_url="https://upload.wikimedia.org/...Signiture_of_Williams.jpg"
image_data = base64.b64encode(httpx.get(image_url).content).decode("utf-8")
...
```

For the interface, we install Streamlit:

```
pip install streamlit
```

We import Streamlit and start with a simple title. Add in **bold**:

```
import anthropic
import base64
import httpx
import streamlit as st

st.title("✒ Handwriting Analyzer")

client = anthropic.Anthropic()
...
```

We can easily use the *title* function of Streamlit to give our site the title "Handwriting Analyzer". To make it a bit more personal, we use a nice emoji ✒.

This below single line starts the user interface:

```
streamlit run app.py
```

```
(venv) (base) MacBook-Air-4:claude user$ streamlit run app.py

  You can now view your Streamlit app in your browser.

  Local URL: http://localhost:8501
  Network URL: http://192.168.18.10:8501
```

and we have a web page with the title:

Next, we add the upload feature by adding the line in **bold**:

```
...
st.title("✏Handwriting Analyzer")

client = anthropic.Anthropic()

uploaded_file = st.file_uploader("Choose a handwriting image",
type=["png","jpg","jpeg"])
...
```

Here we use a file uploader.

Next, when a file is selected, we want to display the uploaded image directly on the web page. For this, we import *Image* from the *PIL* library:

```
import anthropic
import base64
import httpx
import streamlit as st
from PIL import Image
from io import BytesIO
...
```

We also import *Bytes.io* from *io* (explained later).

Add in the following codes in **bold**:

```
...
...
uploaded_file = st.file_uploader("Choose a handwriting image",
type=["png","jpg","jpeg"])
```

```
if uploaded_file is not None:
    image = Image.open(uploaded_file)
    st.image(image, caption="Uploaded Image")

    if st.button("Analyze Handwriting"):
        with st.spinner("Analyzing..."):
            buffered = BytesIO()
            image.save(buffered, format="JPEG")
            image_data = base64.b64encode(buffered.getvalue()).decode()
            message = client.messages.create(
                model="claude-3-5-sonnet-20240620",
                max_tokens=1000,
                messages=[
                    {
                        "role": "user",
                        "content": [
                            {
                                "type": "image",
                                "source": {
                                    "type": "base64",
                                    "media_type": "image/jpeg",
                                    "data": image_data
                                }
                            },
                            {
                                "type": "text",
                                "text": """Analyze handwriting by
observing pressure, size, spacing, slant, baseline, letter shapes, speed,
and length. These factors can reveal personality traits such as emotional
intensity, independence, openness, stability, and ambition.""",
                            }
                        ]
                    }
                ]
            )
            st.subheader("Analysis Results:")
            st.write(message.content[0].text)
```

Note: The code is long, so if you prefer to copy and paste it, contact support@i-ducate.com for the source code

Code Explanation

Although the code is long, the `client.messages.create` call to send the image to the Claude API code is the same as before, except it has been indented under:

70

```
if uploaded_file is not None:
    ...

    if st.button("Analyze Handwriting"):
        with st.spinner("Analyzing..."):
            ...
            message = client.messages.create(
                ...
                ...
            )
```

So the call to Claude is only executed when the user has uploaded an image:

```
if uploaded_file is not None:
    ...
```

and the "Analyze Handwriting" button is clicked.

```
    if st.button("Analyze Handwriting"):
        with st.spinner("Analyzing..."):
            ...
```

We create an in memory byte buffer using BytesIO, *buffered = BytesIO()*:

```
    if st.button("Analyze Handwriting"):
        with st.spinner("Analyzing..."):
            client = anthropic.Anthropic()
            buffered = BytesIO()
            image.save(buffered, format="JPEG")
            image_data = base64.b64encode(buffered.getvalue()).decode()
```

We earlier imported *Bytes.IO* from *io*:

```
...
import streamlit as st
from PIL import Image
from io import BytesIO
```

We save the image into this buffer in JPEG format with *image.save(buffered, format="JPEG")*. Then, the buffer's content is encoded into a base64 string:

```
image_data = base64.b64encode(buffered.getvalue()).decode())
```

This is then sent to the Claude API. In summary, we convert the given uploaded image into a base64 string.

```
    ...
```

```
                    }
                ]
            )
            st.subheader("Analysis Results:")
            st.write(message.content[0].text)
```

We then access *message.content[0]*, the first element of which is the text that contains the analysis.

Running our App

Before running our app, ensure you remove the *print* at the end:
```
print(message.content)
```

Now we have everything we need, and we can go back to the page and try out our image analysis. Let's run our app (*streamlit run app.py*) and upload a handwritten note:

The image is displayed correctly. Let's start the analysis and see the detailed analysis of the image:

Analysis Results:

Based on the handwriting sample in the image, I can provide some general observations about the writing style, but it's important to note that handwriting analysis is not a scientifically validated method for determining personality traits. Here are some observations:

1. Pressure: The writing appears to have medium to heavy pressure, which can suggest confidence and commitment.

2. Size: The writing is relatively large, which might indicate an outgoing nature or desire for attention.

3. Spacing: There's a mix of connected and disconnected letters, which could suggest a balance between logical thinking and intuition.

4. Slant: The writing has a slight right slant, potentially indicating a friendly and outgoing disposition.

5. Baseline: The baseline appears mostly straight, which might suggest stability and consistency.

6. Letter shapes: The writing has a flowing, artistic quality with some embellishments, possibly indicating creativity.

7. Speed: The writing looks fluid and fast, which could suggest quick thinking or impatience.

8. Length: The signature extends across the available space, potentially indicating confidence or expansiveness.

Wonderful, everything worked, and this could be turned into a service where people might be willing to pay a few dollars.

If you have gotten lost at any point, here's the entire code of *app.py*:

```python
import anthropic
import base64
import httpx
import streamlit as st
from PIL import Image
from io import BytesIO

st.title(" Handwriting Analyzer")

client = anthropic.Anthropic()

uploaded_file = st.file_uploader("Choose a handwriting image",
type=["png","jpg","jpeg"])
```

```python
if uploaded_file is not None:
    image = Image.open(uploaded_file)
    st.image(image, caption="Uploaded Image")

    if st.button("Analyze Handwriting"):
        with st.spinner("Analyzing..."):
            buffered = BytesIO()
            image.save(buffered, format="JPEG")
            image_data = base64.b64encode(buffered.getvalue()).decode()
            message = client.messages.create(
                model="claude-3-5-sonnet-20240620",
                max_tokens=1000,
                messages=[
                    {
                        "role": "user",
                        "content": [
                            {
                                "type": "image",
                                "source": {
                                    "type": "base64",
                                    "media_type": "image/jpeg",
                                    "data": image_data
                                }
                            },
                            {
                                "type": "text",
                                "text": """Analyze handwriting by
observing pressure, size, spacing, slant, baseline, letter shapes, speed,
and length. These factors can reveal personality traits such as emotional
intensity, independence, openness, stability, and ambition.""",
                            }
                        ]
                    }
                ]
            )
            st.subheader("Analysis Results:")
            st.write(message.content[0].text)
```

Summary

We have gone through quite a lot of content to equip you with the skills to use Claude effectively.

Hopefully, you have enjoyed this book and would like to learn more from me. I would love to get your feedback, learning what you liked and didn't for us to improve.

Please feel free to email me at support@i-ducate.com if you encounter any errors with your code or to get updated versions of this book.

If you didn't like the book, or if you feel that I should have covered certain additional topics, please email us to let us know. This book can only get better thanks to readers like you. If you like the book, I would appreciate if you could leave us a review too. Thank you and all the best!

About the Author

Greg Lim is a technologist and author of several programming books. Greg has many years in teaching programming in tertiary institutions and he places special emphasis on learning by doing.

Contact Greg at support@i-ducate.com

www.ingramcontent.com/pod-product-compliance
Lightning Source LLC
LaVergne TN
LVHW081531050326
832903LV00025B/1746